THE POPCORN BOOK

Tomie de Paola

THE POPCORN BOOK

SCHOLASTIC INC.
New York Toronto London Auckland Sydney

FOR FLORENCE NESCI,
who taught me how
to pop the best popcorn
in the whole wide world

ISBN 0-590-40264-1

 This edition is published by Scholastic Inc., 730 Broadway, New York, NY 10003, by arrangement with Holiday House, Inc.

19 18 17 16 15 14 13 3 4 5 6 7/9

Printed in the U.S.A. 08

...AND NOW A WORD FROM OUR SPONSOR.

YES, THE POPCORN'S IN THE REFRIGERATOR.
MOM, CAN WE MAKE SOME POPCORN?
YUMMY!
TONY
TINY

I WONDER WHY MOM KEEPS THE POPCORN IN THE REFRIGERATOR?
I DON'T KNOW. I'LL GO LOOK IT UP!
TINY

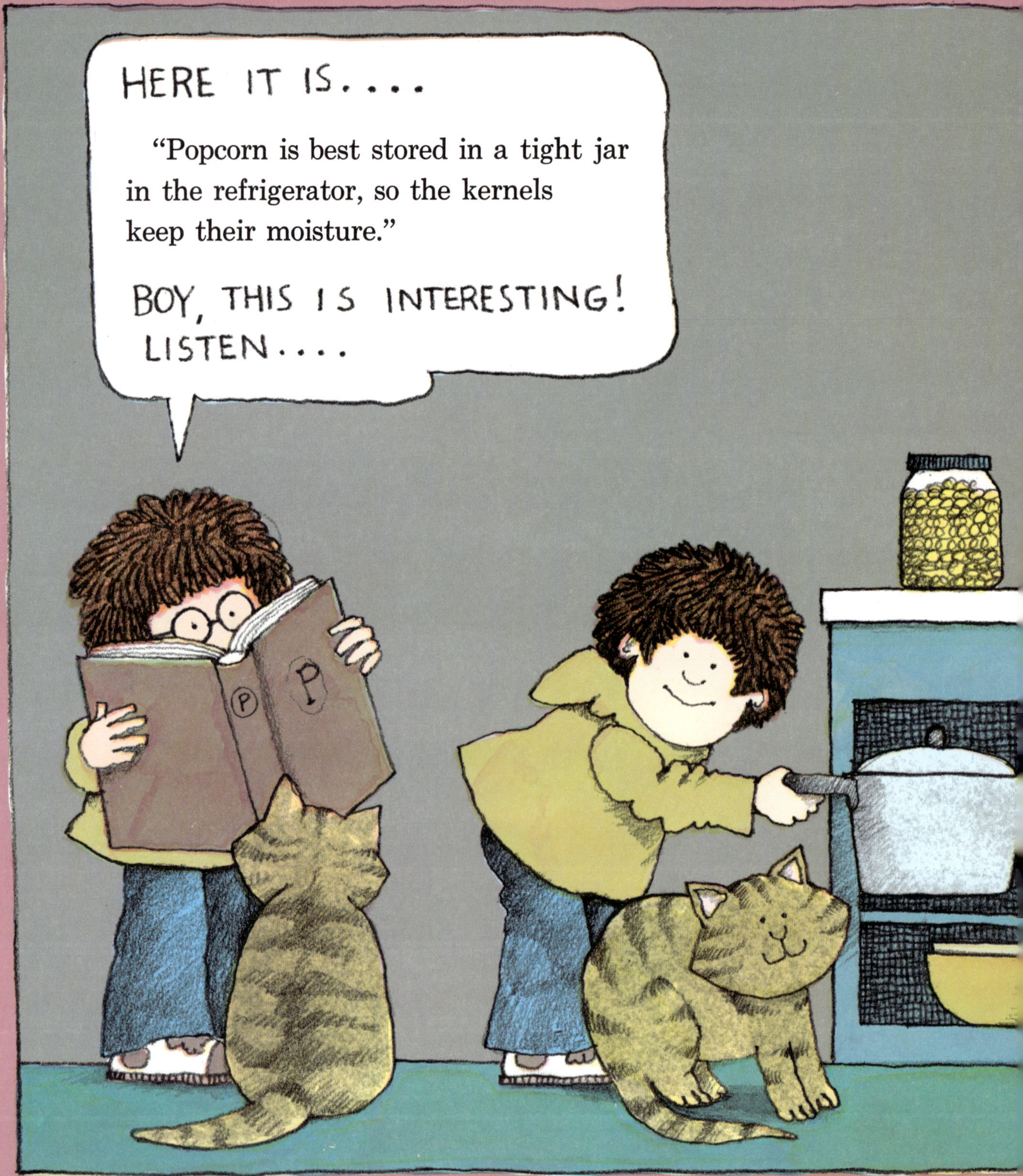

"Popcorn is best stored in a tight jar in the refrigerator, so the kernels keep their moisture."

BOY, THIS IS INTERESTING!
LISTEN....

"Popcorn is the oldest of the three main types of corn. There is field corn, which we feed to animals like cattle and pigs; sweet corn, which is the kind we eat; and popcorn."
COOKING OIL
P
P

"Popcorn was discovered by the Indian people in the Americas many thousands of years ago.

"One of the first sights Columbus saw in the New World was the Indians in San Salvador selling popcorn and wearing it as jewelry."

"But popcorn is even older than that. In a bat cave in New Mexico, archeologists found some popped corn that was 5,600 years old."

"And 1,000-year-old popcorn kernels were found in Peru that could still be popped."

"The Indian people of the Americas had many different ways to pop popcorn.

"One way was to put an ear of corn on a stick and hold it over a fire.

"But many kernels were lost in the fire with this method."

"Another way was to throw the kernels right into the fire by the handful.

"The popcorn popped out all over the place, so there was a lot of bending and running around to gather it up."

“In 1612, French explorers saw some Iroquois people popping corn in clay pots.

“They would fill the pots with hot sand, throw in some popcorn, and stir it with a stick.

“When the corn popped, it came to the top of the sand and was easy to get.”

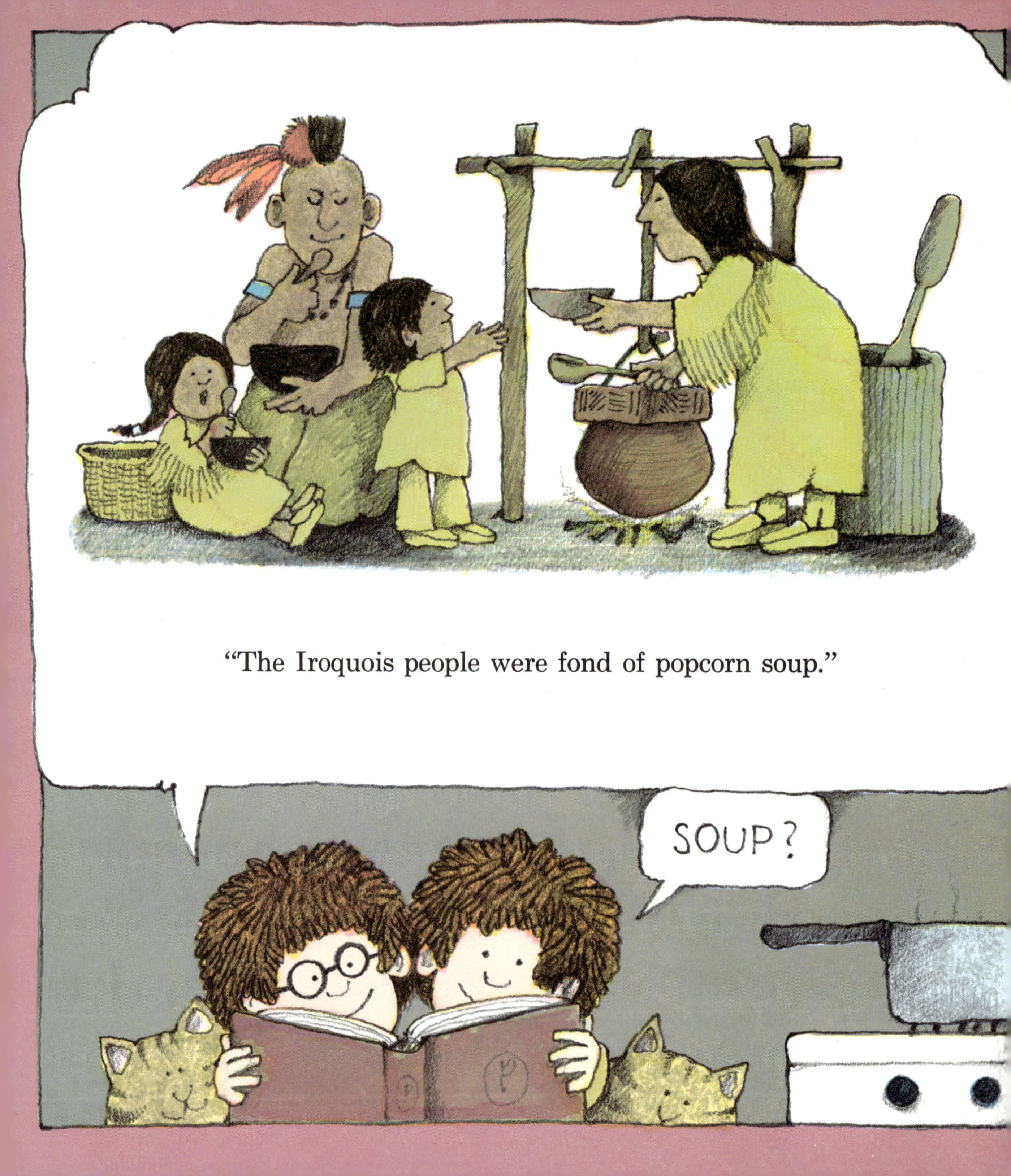

"The Iroquois people were fond of popcorn soup."

“The Algonkians who came to the first Thanksgiving dinner even brought some popcorn in a deerskin pouch.

“The colonists liked it so much that they served popped corn for breakfast with cream poured on it.”

"Today, Americans use 500,000,000 pounds of popcorn each year. 30% is eaten at movies, circuses, ball games, and county fairs. 10% is saved for seed and sold to other countries. But 60% is popped right at home."
OH GOODY, THE KERNELS ARE POPPING. THAT MEANS THE OIL MUST BE READY.

"People in the Midwest buy more popcorn than any other part of the United States.
"Milwaukee and Minneapolis are the top popcorn-eating cities, followed by Chicago and Seattle.
"Most of the popcorn is grown in the Midwest, too."
NOW I'LL PUT MORE KERNELS IN THE PAN AND TURN THE HEAT UP.
P

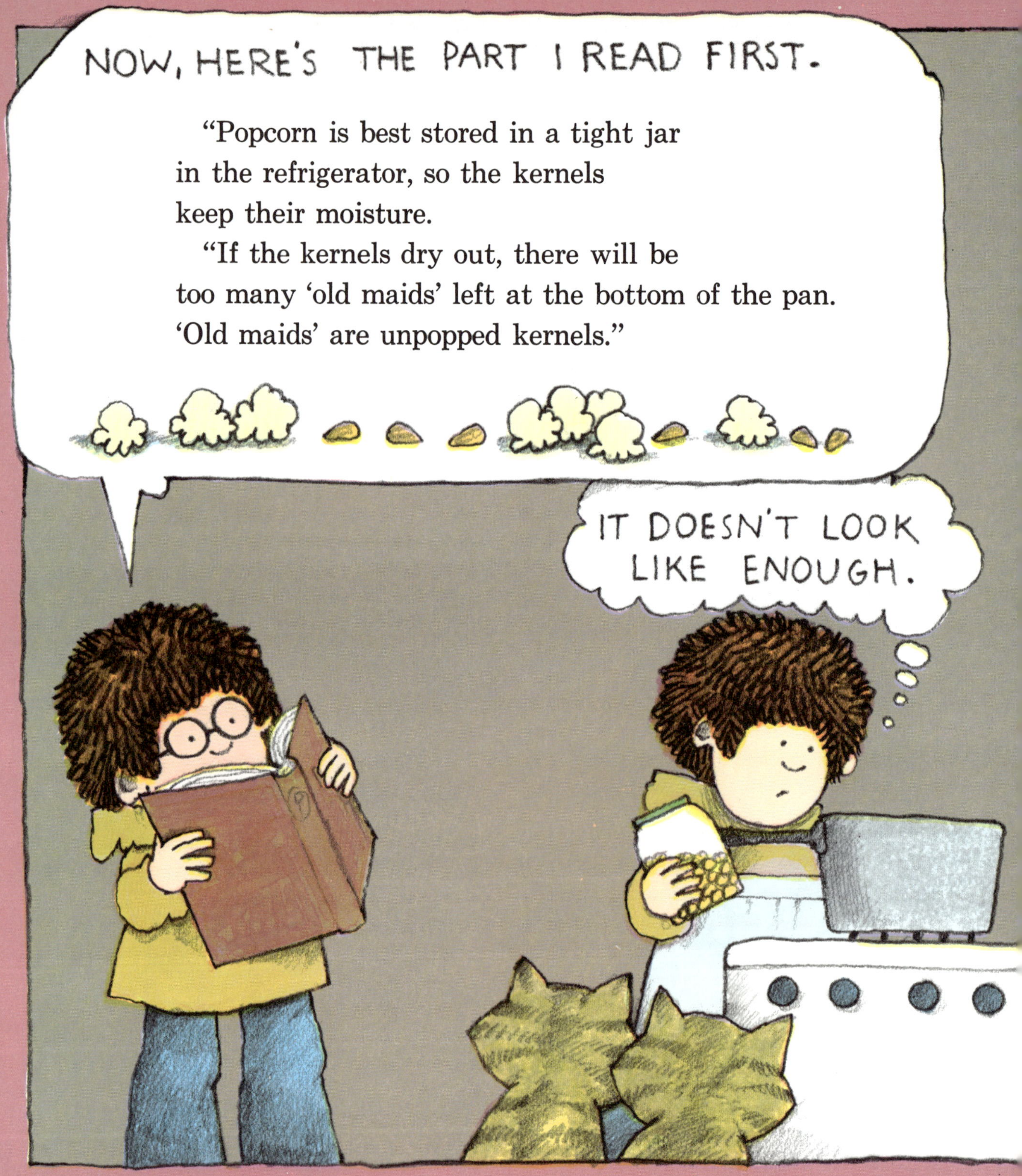

"Popcorn is best stored in a tight jar in the refrigerator, so the kernels keep their moisture.

"If the kernels dry out, there will be too many 'old maids' left at the bottom of the pan. 'Old maids' are unpopped kernels."

"If the popcorn does dry out,
you can add one or two tablespoons of water
to the jar and shake it
until the water is absorbed."
SHAKE
P
P

"Popcorn pops because the heart of the kernel is moist and pulpy and surrounded by a hard starch shell.

"When the kernel is heated, the moisture turns to steam and the heart gets bigger until the shell bursts with a 'pop.' "

ARE YOU SURE YOU DIDNT PUT TOO MUCH POPCORN IN THE PAN ?

OF COURSE NOT, SILLY !

"The Indian people had a legend that inside each kernel of popcorn lived a little demon. When his house was heated, he got so mad that he blew up."

"There are different kinds of popcorn: White hull-less and yellow hull-less are the ones most commonly sold in stores.
"The smallest type is called 'strawberry' because it has red kernels and the ears look like strawberries.
" 'Rainbow' has red, white, yellow, and blue kernels. It is sometimes called 'Calico.'
"There is black popcorn, too, but all of it pops white.
"The biggest kernels are called 'Dynamite' and 'Snow Puff.' "
SHAKE-
SHAKE-
SHAKE-

"After popcorn is popped, most people like to put melted butter and salt on it.

"But if salt is put in the pan before the kernels are popped, it makes the popcorn tough."

"There are many stories about popcorn. One of the funniest and best-known comes from America's Midwest.

One summer, it was so hot and dry that all the popcorn in the fields began to pop.

In no time at all, the sky was filled with flying popcorn.

It looked so much like a blizzard,
everyone put on mittens and scarves
and got out the snow shovels."

HELP! I HAVE A BLIZZARD, TOO!
I KNEW YOU PUT TOO MUCH POPCORN IN THE PAN.

OK, IF YOU'RE SO SMART, WHAT DO WE DO NOW?

I KNOW...

THE BEST THING ABOUT POPCORN.

.IS EATING IT!

TWO TERRIFIC WAYS TO POP CORN

Never make popcorn by yourself. Ask a grown-up or an older child (someone at least 12 years old) to help you. Remember—hot oil can burn!

EVERYDAY WAY

1. Use a heavy 3-quart saucepan that has a cover.
2. Put the pan on the stove. Turn the heat on high for 2 minutes.
3. Pour ¼ cup of cooking oil into the hot pan. The oil should cover the bottom of the pan.
4. Turn the heat down a little. Add 3 or 4 kernels. They will sizzle in the hot oil and then pop.
5. When the 4 kernels pop, add more kernels—enough to cover the bottom of the pan. (Do not use more than ½ cup.)
6. Turn the heat to low and put the cover on the pan. Hold the cover tightly and shake the pan back and forth very fast.
7. When the popping stops, turn the heat off and take the pan away from the stove. Dump the popcorn into a bowl. Pour on some melted butter and sprinkle with salt.
8. Eat!

FRIDAY NIGHT POPCORN
Florence Nesci's recipe

1. Use a large skillet (frying pan) that has a cover.
2. Get a can of vegetable shortening (like Crisco). Scoop out a big spoonful and put it in the skillet.
3. Put the skillet on the stove and turn the heat on low.
4. When the shortening melts, pour in some popcorn kernels—just enough to cover the bottom of the skillet. The melted shortening should come up over the kernels. If it doesn't, add more shortening to the skillet.
5. Now stir the kernels. Stir constantly until 1 or 2 kernels pop. Then put the cover on.
6. Turn the heat up. Hold the cover tightly and shake the skillet. Shake it fast until the popping stops.
7. Pour the popcorn into a bowl and salt it. You don't need any butter.
8. Eat and enjoy it!

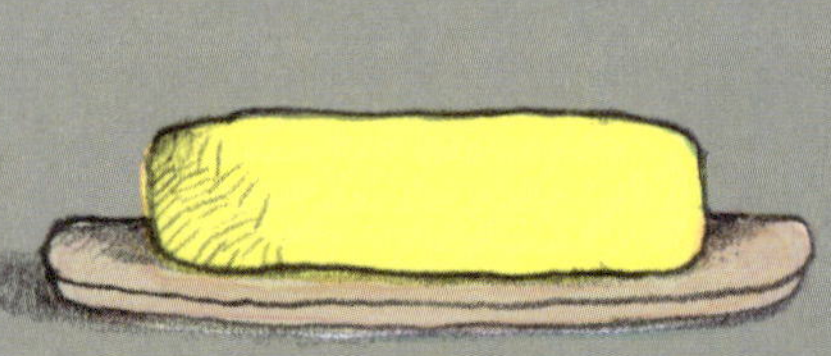

The Itsy Bitsy Spider

The it - sy bit - sy spi-der climbed up the wa - ter - spout.

Down came the rain, and washed the spi - der out!

Out came the sun, and dried up all the rain. And the

it - sy bit - sy spi - der climbed up the spout a - gain.

This time the spider
had climbed the spout prepared!

But the itsy bitsy spider
wasn't one bit scared.

Oh, no! Not again!

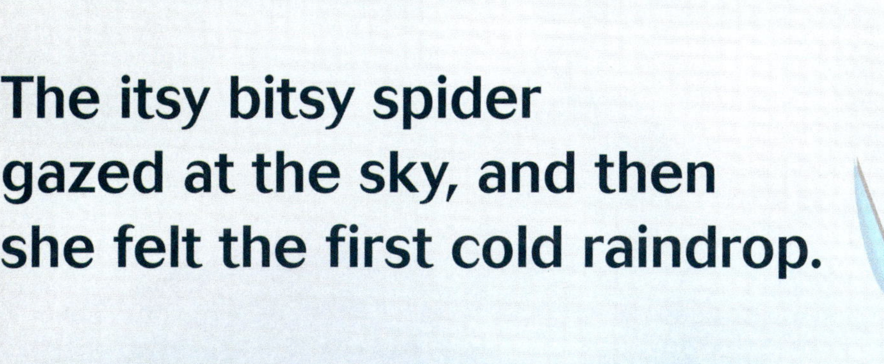

The itsy bitsy spider
gazed at the sky, and then
she felt the first cold raindrop.

. . . the clouds grew
dark with rain,
and covered up the sun.

She spun a silky web,
but just as she was done . . .

The itsy bitsy spider
worked hard all day long,
making a home that
was beautiful and strong.

Then she put down her things
and decided that she'd stay.

She cleaned up the roof,
and she cleared the leaves away.

Up on the rooftop,
the little spider found
a nice sunny spot,
high up above the ground.

And the itsy bitsy spider
climbed up the spout again.

Out came the sun,
and dried up all the rain.

Down came the rain,
and washed the spider out!

The itsy bitsy spider
climbed up the waterspout.

For those who make my dreams come true —
Nana, Jose María, and Alicia.
And especially to Javier and Nina for
making me smile every morning.
— C.B.

ISBN 978-0-545-27570-5

12 11 10 9 8 7 6 5 4 3 2 1 10 11 12 13 14 15/0

Printed in the U.S.A. 40

First printing, October 2010
Book design by Kevin Callahan

The Itsy Bitsy Spider

Illustrated by Constanza Basaluzzo

Scholastic Inc.
New York Toronto London Auckland
Sydney Mexico City New Delhi Hong Kong